An African Mother Christmas

Gcina Mhlophe **Alzette Prins**

I would like to dedicate this book with love to all South African children who do not have anyone to give them presents at Christmas. (G.M.)

My name is Thando and I live in the Valley of a Thousand Hills. I am nine years old, and my brother Buntu is twelve. My name, Thando, means *love* and my brother's name, Buntu, means *humanity*. Our father says that he and our mother gave us those names because they love people. I like that.

When I look outside the village where we live, I see the thousand hills like one big family. Our house is on top of one of the hills and below us are many other houses, far below into the green valley. The vegetable gardens around the houses make neat, green patterns across the land.

Our house is made of mud bricks and it has four rooms. The corrugated iron roof is painted green. The walls are decorated with clay colours like cream, white, red, orange and black. My mother paints the walls herself with folded pieces of sheepskin instead of a brush – and Buntu and I help. We like helping with this job.

December is a very hot month in our valley. We children get so hot from running and playing in the sun, that later we just fall into the river to swim and cool down. We cannot sleep late because the sun is so strong even before it really comes up. Early morning is a good time. I like to sit quietly while I wake up and watch the morning sky and listen to the birds.

December is also a very busy month. People start to come home from the places where they work in big cities. Everybody looks forward to Christmas.

Last year Baba bought a new dining-room table and six new chairs. We helped Mama put new paint on all the walls and everything looked new and fresh. Each morning Buntu and I picked flowers to put in a pot on the new table and everyone was happy. Our house felt brand new.

Then it was time to go to the city to buy new clothes. We went on the train and there were many other children, all going to town for the same thing. Everyone was very excited. This is the only time many of us get any new clothes or presents.

When we got to the city it was very hot. I wanted to take off my shoes and socks, but the pavement was much too hot! I was hoping with all my heart for a new doll with a pretty little dress. There were so many beautiful toys and clothes in the shops we went to. I wished I could just buy and buy, even for our cousins at home. We tried on clothes and shoes and looked at ourselves in the mirror. We had a wonderful time, but suddenly we were very tired.

Baba said he would buy us ice-creams. I could not stop smiling. I looked at Buntu and I knew we were the happiest children in the whole of Durban!

Then, just as we were walking to the train station, carrying all our parcels, we saw the funniest-looking man in the world. He was wearing a red and white winter suit, black boots and a red and white hat, and he had a fluffy white beard. He looked so strange on this hot Durban day that Buntu and I burst out laughing.

'Why is that man dressed like that on such a hot day?' Buntu asked.

'He must be very sweaty inside that suit,' I said. 'Who is he?'

Mama looked at us, trying to hide her laughter. 'He is a kind man who gives children Christmas presents, so don't laugh at him,' she said.

'But Mama, why has he never given *us* any presents?' I asked.

'Oh Thando, he would if he could. But he doesn't know where we live,' Mama replied.

Buntu tried to make his way through the crowd. 'We must tell him right now!' he said.

Baba quickly pulled him away. 'I don't think so Buntu. The old man is very busy right now, and it is too far for him to travel all the way to the Valley of a Thousand Hills!'

When we got back home, Mama gave us the big mangoes we had bought in the city. They were delicious. I don't know what I would do if I woke up one morning and someone told me there were no more mangoes in the world. I love the smell, the taste – and the feeling I get after I eat a mango!

But then I was not so happy any more. We washed our hands and faces. We admired our new clothes, but something was wrong. I still did not understand why that man called Father Christmas never brought us any presents. How could he go to other children's homes and not to ours? It wasn't fair!

Mama realized how upset I was. She sat next to me and tried to comfort me. Buntu was there too. Mama asked him if he was also angry and he said, 'No. We have enjoyed Christmas with everyone in our village every year. We had never heard of Father Christmas before and we were fine. So I think we can still have a wonderful time.'

When my brother said that, I think something inside me became a little hopeful. I don't know what I was hopeful about. I just badly wanted to believe that something really special was going to happen that year.

I wanted Christmas to come quickly. I couldn't wait. Everything was moving very slowly. With every passing day I became more excited.

Then I remembered a story our grandmother had once told us. The story was about a beautiful rain goddess called Nomkhubulwana. Gogo said that Nomkhubulwana was a goddess of fertility and purity. People believed that she had magical powers to make things grow. In the long-ago time, young girls would go and plant a garden for her up on the mountains. She loved the Valley of a Thousand Hills as it was her home in the years when there were not so many people living there. There was always a magical, misty blanket covering Nomkhubulwana wherever she went. And she loved children.

Suddenly I knew in my heart that the goddess would come and play with the children in my village. My heart told me that she would teach us happy new songs or even bring us little gifts. I closed my eyes and tried so hard to imagine what she would look like. But I could not.

The night before Christmas I told Buntu what I was secretly hoping for.

'Oh Thando, it would be so wonderful if she could come. That would make our valley the most special valley in the whole of South Africa.' I saw a light shining in my brother's eyes and I knew he wanted this miracle to happen just as much as I did.

While we were talking, it started to rain. There was lightning and thunder – so loud our house seemed to shake. I prayed that it was a good-luck rain preparing everything for the special day. We fell asleep with the rain still pouring.

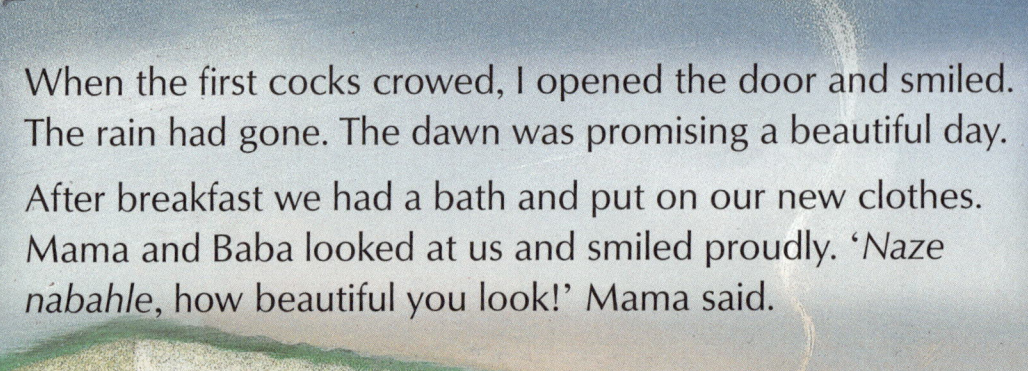

When the first cocks crowed, I opened the door and smiled. The rain had gone. The dawn was promising a beautiful day.

After breakfast we had a bath and put on our new clothes. Mama and Baba looked at us and smiled proudly. '*Naze nabahle*, how beautiful you look!' Mama said.

Then we heard the children in the houses below our home shouting something again and again. They sounded so happy we turned and ran down the hill. As we got closer we heard a strange sound like that of a horn being blown.

And then, slowly moving through the banana patch, we saw the strangest sight, the most wonderful sight I had ever seen. It was a huge grey elephant trumpeting loudly and happily. On his back was a beautiful woman.

I could not open my eyes wide enough to see everything. She was wearing an orange and blue summer dress and leather sandals. A beautiful beaded necklace hung around her neck and she wore matching earrings and bangles.

She had a wonderful hairstyle – her hair was in coils like little snakes, one coil came down to just between her eyes with a sea shell at the end of it. Her face was a golden honey colour and she was tall. She also carried a large leather bag – could it be full of presents?

My wish had come true. I thought I would burst with pride and joy. I could not even jump and shout 'Mother Christmas!' with the other children. I just stood there and smiled and smiled.

She came down to greet us. She was so very pretty. Her smile was like no other I had ever seen before. She opened her bag and looked at us with teasing eyes. Out came a little doll that looked exactly like her, then another and then another. She gave us dolls and toy elephants. Necklaces and clay bowls. Bamboo flutes and drums.

We were all so happy we started running around the elephant chanting, '*Siyabonga, siyabonga MasoKhisimusi, Siyabonga Ndlovu enhle!*' That means, '*Thank you, thank you Mother Christmas, thank you beautiful elephant!*'

One of the girls ran into a house and fetched some water for Mother Christmas to drink. Mother Christmas shared it with her elephant. Then she got back onto the elephant and waved goodbye.

She left us standing there, holding our gifts. Would our parents believe us when we told them what we had seen? I knew that she was the rain goddess of fertility – Nomkhubulwana. I knew my grandmother would believe me.

I think Nomkhubulwana will come back again. I can't wait to find out.